ROMANCING THE SHORE:
Views of Coastal New England

A LOAN EXHIBITION

May 13 through October 14, 1990

HERITAGE PLANTATION OF SANDWICH
Brian Cullity, Curator

Lenders to Romancing the Shore

Addison Gallery of American Art, Andover, MA

Art Complex Museum, Duxbury, MA

The Baltimore Museum of Art, Baltimore, MD

The Bostonian Society, Boston, MA

Mr. Morton Bradley, Arlington, MA

The Brooklyn Museum, Brooklyn, NY

The Butler Institute, Youngstown, OH

The Cahoon Museum of American Art, Cotuit, MA

Cape Ann Historical Society, Gloucester, MA

Centerville Historical Society, Centerville, MA

Child's Gallery, Inc., Boston, MA

Sterling and Francine Clark Art Institute,
    Williamstown, MA

The Corcoran Gallery, Washington, DC

Essex Institute, Salem, MA

Fruitlands Museum, Harvard, MA

George Walter Vincent Smith Art Museum,
    Springfield, MA

Georgia Museum of Art, Athens, GA

Heckscher Museum, Huntington, NY

The Historical Society of Pennsylvania,
    Philadelphia, PA

Indianapolis Museum of Art, Indianapolis, IN

Peter and Carolyn Lynch, Marblehead, MA

Lynn Historical Society, Lynn, MA

Milwaukee Art Museum, Milwaukee, WI

Museum of Fine Arts, Boston, MA

Mystic Seaport Museum, Inc., Mystic, CT

Nantucket Historical Association, Nantucket, MA

Newport Art Museum, Newport, RI

Peabody Museum, Salem, MA

Portland Museum of Art, Portland, ME

Provincetown Art Association & Museum,
    Provincetown, MA

Rhode Island Historical Society, Providence, RI

Dr. R.M. Rowe, South Dennis, MA

San Diego Museum of Art, San Diego, CA

Sandwich Historical Society, Sandwich, MA

George Walter Vincent Smith Art Museum,
    Springfield, MA

Syracuse University Art Collection, Syracuse, NY

Whitney Museum of American Art, New York, NY

Woods Hole Historical Society, Woods Hole, MA

Woods Hole Library, Woods Hole, MA

Cover photo:
"A September Day on the Coast"
by Francis Silva
Collection of Peter and Carolyn Lynch
Cat. #92

Title page photo:
Coast of Grand Manan
by Alfred Bricher
Collection of Mr. Morton Bradley
Cat. #8

ISBN 0-939059-05-3

This catalogue has been made possible, in part, by grants from Peter and Carolyn Lynch, Marblehead,
Massachusetts and Franklin Graphics, Providence, Rhode Island.

FOREWORD

New Englanders have a special interest in marine paintings and ship portraits. Maritime industry and commerce have been a vital part of our history and growth and paintings provide us with a visual aid to this past. The sea is also a source of romance, awe and inspiration, serving as a constant reminder of our transient nature. The coast, where the land meets the sea, is the link to the vastness of the ocean — an emotional link — that has been the inducement of countless attempts to capture its essence and spirit on canvas. This exhibit surveys those attempts and shares with the viewer the efforts artists have made over the years to explore that union between the ocean and the land. It also shares a view of a time when one could find unsullied beaches and coves, free from the pollutants of the twentieth century and will, perhaps, contribute in a small way to the determined effort to cleanse our shores.

The selection of paintings in the show cover two centuries of American marine art history and are but a representative sampling of examples that can be found on the subject. A special effort has been made to include works and artists germane to southeastern New England in addition to a wider variety of subjects and methods of painting. American landscape painting has always fallen into phases; the changes in style reflective of society's subjective interest. This exhibit chronicles those phases with a presentation of ship portraits, traditional coastal views, genre, narrative, impressionist and other representative works.

ROMANCING THE SHORE
INTRODUCTION

"The painter of American scenery has, indeed, privileges superior to any other. All nature here is new to art . . ." Although Thomas Cole was writing those lines specifically about the Catskill Mountains in 1835, he could just as well have been speaking of all America or the New England coast. The rocky, wave beaten shores, sandy dunes, superb harbors and serene marshes are but a few of the scores of changing scenes to be found on New England's 2,000 miles of coastline. The perpetual motion and energy of the ocean and continually changing spectrum of colors of the land and sky have provided a natural and compelling subject for the artist since the beginning of landscape painting in America, two hundred years ago.

Read any history of American marine painting and you will repeatedly encounter the word romantic or a derivative – and for obvious reasons. Historically, artists have depicted the New England coast using a variety of techniques ranging from realism to modernism, but always with a romantic vision that seeks to establish a union between nature and the human spirit. This is the thread that provides the continuity for the artistic diversity and range of expertise to be found in the two centuries of New England coastal painting.

It is difficult to imagine a period in American art history devoid of landscape paintings, in particular, coastal views. However, prior to the late eighteenth century, the landscape was usually relegated to the secondary role of background in portraiture work or occasionally as an overmantle painting. The smattering of early marines to be found in this period are mostly topographical, fantasy or historical works by West, Allston, Corne or Shaw. The advent of the Romantic movement in the late eighteenth century contributed to an artistic and literary adoration of nature. It was felt that the contemplation and appreciation of nature would soothe and uplift the soul. Moreover, in this country, the search for self-identity following Independence, resulted in a demand for a culture and art that was distinctly American. The lack of picturesque ruins and the artistic traditions of Europe were deplored by writers and artists but America's unspoiled, vast wilderness and coastline provided an alternative source for painting and literature.

Changing American attitude by the 1820's gave rise to the success of landscape and marine artists. Thomas Birch, Alvan Fisher and Thomas Doughty were among the pioneers of this period; however, their work was in the English landscape tradition. Thomas Cole and his followers pursued different aims than their European counterparts which we now label as the Hudson River School of painting. The scope of the Hudson River School is wider than the name implies — for the work was certainly not limited to the Hudson River region. Indeed, Hudson River School is not a school at all, rather it describes the use of light to capture a dramatic effect in landscapes. The artists retained European compositional formats but utilized the vastness of American geography to create panoramic landscapes with vivid color schemes and rich textures.

The second generation of the Hudson River School found the New England coast an ideal setting for their work. Kensett, Lane, Heade, Bradford, Church, Richards, Haseltine and the Moran brothers are but a few of the artists whose works frequently are identified with the New England seacoast. These middle decades also found a growing fascination with light, both scientifically and artistically. This fascination was often interpreted on canvas by a gentle golden glow of sunlight through a mist filled atmosphere. This exploration of light and atmosphere in art has been labeled "Luminism" and is a natural progression from, but not apart of, the Hudson River School.

Marine painting during this period was secondary to the epic landscapes of Cole and his contemporaries; however, the importance of maritime trade and commerce to New England was reflected in the demand for ship portraits and harbor views during the early nineteenth century. The detailed paintings of Robert Salmon provided scores of artists with a successful model to emulate. These harbor views are not only aesthetically pleasing, but they provide us with important historical documents of the activity in urban ports. This very commercial activity however, may have provided the inspiration for artists to search out the more remote coastal areas of New England for the idealized romantic subject to paint. Fisher, Doughty and Birch, along with other early Hudson River artists sought untouched areas of New England shore as subject matter for their canvases, although they produced only a handful of paintings in the beginning. The next generation of painters would soon flood galleries and collectors with romantic, glowing versions of the New England coast.

The Dutch marine tradition had profound influence on American art in the early nineteenth century. The style, fully developed by the late seventeenth century in Holland, was to have a considerable impact on the English seascapist. They in turn taught other generations of English artists who would eventually immigrate to America. Robert Salmon, Thomas Birch and James Buttersworth were all born and trained in Great Britain and later lived and worked in America. Holland was the source of the Dutch artists Albert Van Beest and the deHaas brothers, William and Mauritz, who would also immigrate a few years later. The influence of these men on American marine art is obvious when a Fitz Hugh Lane painting is compared to a Salmon, or a Bradford painting to a Van Beest. A low horizon, concentration on light and air, detailed execution of ship elements and a distinct manner of portraying the rippling effect of waves characterizes the influence of the Dutch marine school.

The years following the Civil War saw the decline in popularity of landscapes in the Hudson River style. The influence of the Dusseldorf school in Germany and the French Barbizon painters was beginning to appear in the work of American artists who had traveled to Europe. This transition can be seen in the art of George Inness. His early work is distinctly of the Hudson River style but adapts to the tastes of the more atmospheric French Barbizon artists following several tours of Europe. Inness stated it succinctly: "The purpose of the painter is simply to reproduce in other minds the impression which a scene has made upon him . . . Its aim is not to instruct, not to edify, but to awaken an emotion . . ."

Nature, for the Barbizon painters, was not forgotten, only reinterpreted. The grand, panoramic views were abandoned in favor of quiet landscapes virtually devoid of the human figure. A looser brushwork is characteristic and a tonal quality is apparent in many of the works of artists who received training in France. William Morris Hunt, John Enneking and William Gay are three of the finest proponents of this expression in American art.

Many of these students returned to America and made significant contributions to the development of art in the realist tradition. There were some notable exceptions who chose to remain in Europe, namely Mary Cassatt, John Singer Sargent and James Abbott MacNeill Whistler. The combined influence of the expatriates, the Barbizon School, Dusseldorf and Impressionism helped to create a unique American style of painting which would culminate in the genre and landscape works of Homer and Eakins. The close of the nineteenth century saw the direction of landscape painting turn towards Impressionism. The interest in light and its sources had begun with the Luminists, developed with the Realists and was brought to fruition by the Impressionists. Their works were characterized by a brighter, more intensely saturated palette and the purposeful introduction of brushwork to the texture of the painting. Much of the painting was accomplished out of doors (au plein air) — a technique that was developed and refined by the French Barbizon painters (this was possible only after the development of the collapsible tin tube to hold premixed oil paints in 1841). Unlike their European counterparts; however, American Impressionists strove to enrich and enliven their subject with color and light, not to reduce all form to patches of color. American artists retained a strong grasp on Realism throughout this period, even those that

most closely resembled the French Impressionists. The most influential group of American Impressionists were called the Ten and included Childe Hassam, Twatchman, Chase and Robinson. They held annual exhibits of their work from 1898 until 1906 — about the time the Ashcan movement began to make significant changes in American art.

The leader of the Ashcan School was Robert Henri. He, along with John Sloan, Glackens, Davies, Prendergast, Lawson, Shinn and Luks formed a group of artists called the Eight as a revolt against the "genteel" images of American art — especially that produced by the Ten. The Eight were champions of the American scene and sought to depict images of truth. They felt subject matter should reflect the commonplace and have a social relevance. As Henri stated, "Draw your material from the life around you, all of it. There is beauty in everything if it looks beautiful to your eyes. You can find it anywhere, everywhere." Many of these works depict urban life and focus on slum and industrial images. Wharves, docks, decaying factories and the people who inhabited them were the subjects for these artists. The realism of this group entered new and adventurous ground which was democratic and appealing to the public, but not to the conservative National Academy of Design. Consequently, the younger New York Realists rebelled against the National Academy and held an independent exhibition of their own work now known as the famous Armory Show of 1913. The exhibit included almost five hundred European works and one thousand from American artists; a most significant display of contemporary work that presaged the more radical modernism and abstract art to appear in years to follow.

The early twentieth century also saw the establishment of a number of art schools and colonies in New England, most devoted to land and seascape painting. Old Lyme, Provincetown, Ogunquit, Gloucester and Rockport are but a few of the influential groups formed during this period which continue to this day. Most were proponents of au plein air painting and found the coast of New England offered outstanding opportunities for subject matter.

Perhaps the most difficult of all the styles of marine painting to classify and describe is that of the folk artist, yet they often produced some of the most timeless depictions to be found in American art. Working with a bold, linear manner, the folk tradition has occasionally been close to the mainstream of artistic development, but more often followed its own path. The resulting images are frequently startling perceptions by the untrained artist, and almost always compelling. Many are by anonymous artists, or, if we do have a name, we know nothing about them. Their common goal however, was the same as all artists and it is this aesthetic that we appreciate today as much as when it was first created.

THE CATALOGUE

DAVID MAITLAND ARMSTRONG
1836-1918

David Armstrong was born in New York, at Danskammer, the family estate overlooking the Hudson River, April 15, 1836. He attended Trinity College in Hartford, Connecticut and Harvard Law School and was admitted to the bar in 1862. He had made a trip to Europe in 1858 and was later appointed consul to the Papal States in 1869. This position enabled him to become friendly with many of the local American artists in Rome including William Haseltine, Charles Coleman, George Healy and Elihu Vedder. They in turn, exerted an effect on his artistic work and he eventually gave up the consular post in 1872 to devote full time to his painting. Armstrong exhibited at the National Academy and the Brooklyn Art Association throughout the 1870's but turned to stained glass designing in the early 1880's. He worked for both Tiffany and LaFarge before establishing his own company in the early 1890's. Armstrong died in 1918 in New York City.

1. **The Bar, Bar Harbor, Mount Desert,** *1883*
   Oil on canvas, 24⅛" x 47⅛"
   Signed l.r. "The Bar-Bar Harbor/Mount Desert/Maitland Armstrong 1883"
   Collection of Milwaukee Museum of Art, Gift of Frederick Layton (L1916.13)

   This work was probably painted after the artist's trip to Maine in the summer of 1876 and exhibited at the National Academy in 1877. The painting was reworked by Armstrong in 1883.

THOMAS HART BENTON
1889-1975

Thomas Hart Benton has been described as the leading exponent of regionalism in the United States. As such, it is appropriate that his family roots were firmly established in Missouri tradition and history. Benton attended classes at the Corcoran gallery of Art in Washington, D.C. at a time when his father was serving in the House of Representatives. Benton later studied Cubism at the Academie Julian in Paris. Benton's sinuous and colorful compositions of rural, mid-western life are perhaps his best known works; however, his frequent summer retreats to the Massachusetts island of Martha's Vineyard were equally productive — coastal views and Yankee natives replacing the midwestern plains and country folk. Benton died in Kansas City, Missouri in 1975.

2. **Chilmark,** *c. 1920*
   Watercolor on paper, 13" x 17"
   Signed l.l. "Benton"
   Collection of The Butler Institute of Amercian Art

   A letter from Benton dated April 9, 1970, comments on this painting: "The subject is now quite different. The trees have so grown that the house is no more visible nor is most of the lower section of water visible any more."

1.

2.

THOMAS BIRCH
1779-1851

Thomas Birch was born in England in 1779 and came to this country with his father, the noted engraver and miniaturist, William Russell Birch, in 1794. Together they published a portfolio of engraved views of the city of Philadelphia in 1799-1800 as William Birch and Son. Thomas became a most prolific artist noted for his landscapes and marine views and was soon elected to the Pennsylvania Academy of Fine Arts. Birch documented much of the Eastern coast of the United States employing techniques commonly found in Dutch marine paintings of the period. He showed great concern for accuracy and "naturalistic representation" which brought him much praise and many patrons; however, his greatest contribution was making "marine painting American by treating local subject matter with a personal, independent style. His paintings are individually valuable as historical documents." Birch died in Philadelphia in 1851 after a long and successful career as a marine painter.

3. Off The Maine Coast, *1835*
Oil on canvas, 39½" x 59½"
Signed l.r. "Thom. Birch 1835"
Collection of Fruitland Museums

John Wilmerding cites this painting as clearly showing the influence of the French romantic seascapist, Vernet. The formula of high rocky cliffs cutting off one side of the canvas on a diagonal with a ship foundering offshore and survivors struggling amidst wreckage was used effectively by this eighteenth century Romantic painter.

4. Minot's Ledge Rock Light, *c. 1830's*
Oil on canvas, 19¾" x 29⅞"
Unsigned
Collection of the Historical Society of Pennsylvania

This dramatic scene of a stormy rescue is Birch at his best; however, the title of this painting is misleading since the lighthouse at Minot's Ledge (that resembles the one in the painting) wasn't built until nine years after Birch's death. It is not known which lighthouse this painting actually portrays.

5. Panorama of Nantucket Town Across the Harbor, *c. 1810*
Oil on canvas, 22" x 31¾"
Unsigned
Collection of Nantucket Historical Association (74.21)

There is a strong possibility that this painting was executed from the engraving "The Town of Sherburne in the Island of Nantucket" published around 1811 by Benjamin Tanner and sketched by Joseph Sansom.

3.

4.

5.

GERTRUDE BEALS BOURNE
1867-1962

Gertrude Bourne was raised in the Back Bay of Boston and received private art lessons from Henry Rice and Henry B. Snell (one of the founding members of the New York Watercolor Club). She made several trips to Europe with her family in the 1890's, painting in Norway, France and England. Her work from this period has been compared with the American landscape realists Childe Hassam and Winslow Homer. Bourne established a studio in her Beacon Street house early in the twentieth century and maintained it until her death at age ninety-five. She also continued to exhibit both nationally and locally until the age of eighty-eight. Much of her work is of the North Shore where she and her family summered from about 1911 on. Bourne died in 1962.

6. Sailboats on the North Shore, c. 1895
Watercolor on paper, 12½" x 18½"
Signed on reverse with estate stamp
Collection of Childs Gallery, Boston and New York

The stylistic relationship to Homer is quite evident in this watercolor of the North Shore.

WILLIAM BRADFORD
1823-1892

William Bradford was born in Fairhaven, near New Bedford, Massachusetts, April 25, 1823. He worked as a shopkeeper prior to his decision to turn to painting in 1854. In that year he invited the Dutch marine painter, Albert Van Beest, to come to New Bedford and instruct him in return for room, board and studio space. His first exhibition was at the National Academy in 1860. Later, from 1861 to 1867, Bradford made several voyages to Labrador and the Artic and consequently became well known for his dramatic paintings of those regions. In addition to the National Academy, Bradford exhibited at the Boston Athenaeum and the Royal Academy of London. He died in New York City in 1892 while on a lecture visit.

7. Lynn Beach, *nd*
Oil on canvas, 11" x 20"
Unsigned, attributed to William Bradford
Collection Lynn Historical Society (2029)

This view depicts a broad expanse of the beach by the industrial city of Lynn during the mid-nineteenth century and is quite similar to another Bradford painting in the collection of Indiana University Art Museum.

6.

7.

ALFRED THOMPSON BRICHER
1837-1908

The noted land and seascape painter, Alfred Bricher, appears to have been self-taught. He was born in Portsmouth, New Hampshire on April 10, 1837 but moved with his family at an early age to Newburyport, Massachusetts. He was initially employed as a clerk in a Boston business but had opened an art studio by the time he was only twenty-one. He made numerous trips throughout New England and New York for subject matter and turned increasingly towards the sea for his compositions. His works are carefully balanced, luminous paintings that exhibit great attention to detail. Bricher moved his studio to New York City in 1868 and was elected an Associate of the National Academy in 1879. The artist died in New Dorp, Staten Island on September 30, 1908.

8. **Coast of Grand Manan,** *nd*
Oil on canvas, 38" X 27¾"
Signed l.l. "A.T. Bricher"
Collection of Mr. Morton Bradley
Illustrated on title page.

9. **Morning at Grand Manan,** *1878*
Oil on canvas, 25" x 50"
Signed l.l. "A.T. Bricher, 1878"
© 1990 Indianapolis Museum of Art,
Martha Delzell Memorial Fund (70.65)
Illustrated Plate I

Bricher is noted for his depictions of the coast of Maine and the luminous atmosphere they exhibit such as seen in these two wonderful paintings. Grand Manan is actually an island that belongs to Canada but is only eight miles off the Maine coast. The island has been a favorite subject for many marine painters of the nineteenth century because of its dramatic coastline.

GEORGE LORING BROWN
1814-1889

George Loring Brown was a noted landscape, portrait and miniature painter, lithographer, etcher and wood engraver who was born in Boston, February 2, 1814. His early training was as an apprentice to Alonso Hartwell, a wood engraver. At the encouragement of G.P.A. Healy, he went to Europe to study painting in 1831. After his return to Boston in 1834, he resumed the career of engraving, only to leave again for Europe in 1840, spending the next twenty years there. Brown exhibited his work frequently at the Boston Athenaeum, the National Academy and the Pennsylvania Academy. He died in Malden, Massachusetts in 1889.

10. **Boston From an Island in the Harbor,** *1839*
Oil on canvas, 21" x 26"
Signed l.c. "G.L. Brown 1839"
Collection of The Bostonian Society (12.18)

This view of Boston and its new State House, appears to have been taken from either Thompson's or Spectacle Island looking northwest.

HARRISON B. BROWN
1831-1915

Harrison Brown was born in Portland, Maine in 1831 and began his career as a sign and banner painter in that city; however, he was exhibiting landscapes at the National Academy by 1858. His later work also included marine paintings. Brown moved to England in 1892 and died in London, March 27, 1915.

11. **H.M.S. Monarch off the Portland Light,** *1870*
Oil on canvas, 18" x 32¼"
Signed l.l. "H.B. Brown 1870"
Collection of Peabody Museum of Salem (2045)

The H.M.S. Monarch was built in Chatham, England 1866-1869. This painting shows the vessel off the Portland light with American vessels escorting her in the background.

10.

11.

AUGUSTUS WALDECK BUHLER
1853-1920

Augustus Buhler was the son of political refugees from the Prussian province of Silesia. He was born in New York City on September 30, 1853 and moved to Worcester, Massachusetts when he was twelve. Buhler took art lessons in Worcester, at the Boston Art Club (under Tommaso Juglaris) and the Rhode Island School of Design before leaving for France in 1888. He studied at the Ecole des Beaux Arts and Academie Julian and returned to this country in 1890. He was an illustrator for several periodicals and sold paintings to the Brown and Bigelow Company for use as calendar illustrations. Many of Buhler's paintings were of Gloucester fishermen and the marine environment of the North Shore area. He died in Gloucester in 1920.

12. Rocks in Sunlight, *1914*
Oil on canvas, 8¾" x 11¾"
Signed l.r. "A.W. Buhler 14"
Collection of Cape Ann Historical Association (2466)

13. Sandy Dunes, Annisquam Lighthouse, *1915*
Oil on canvas, 8¾" x 11¾"
Signed l.r. "A.W. Buhler" 1915
Collection of Cape Ann Historical Association (2466)

14. Coming Around Annisquam, *c. 1915*
Oil on wood, 9" x 12"
Signed l.l. "A.W. Buhler"
Collection of Cape Ann Historical Association (2466)

15. Smith's Cove, *c. 1915*
Oil on canvas, 9" x 12"
Signed l.l. "A.W. Buhler"
Collection of Cape Ann Historical Association (2466)

2.

13.

4.

15.

WILLIAM PARTRIDGE BURPEE
1846-1940

William Partridge Burpee, who was born in Rockland, Maine, April 13, 1846, started his career as a clerk in the city of Boston, Massachusetts. He studied with the noted marine painter, William Bradford, in the 1870's and by 1885 was an accomplished coastal painter himself. His paintings of Lynn Beach with children playing or lobstermen, dorymen, netmenders and others attending to the business of making a living are quite similar to Bradford's views of the same beach done thirty years earlier. Burpee's paintings show more of an impressionist style after his extended tour of Europe from 1896-1899 and also reflect his interest in tonalism. Much of his later work was confined to pastel views of the Palisades overlooking the Hudson River. He died in Rockland, Maine in 1940.

16. Beach Scene With Clouds and Rain, *c. 1880*
Oil on paper, mounted on board, 7¼" x 10⅝"
Unsigned
Collection of Childs Gallery, Boston and New York

17. Boy on Beach, *c. 1885-90*
Oil on canvasboard, 10" x 13¼"
Unsigned
Collection of Childs Gallery, Boston and New York

18. Coastal Scene With Ships, *c. 1905*
Oil on mahogany panel, 6" x 8½"
Unsigned
Collection of Childs Gallery, Boston and New York

19. Fisherman With Wheelbarrow and Dory on Beach, *c. 1885-90*
Oil on paper, mounted on mahogany board, 7½" x 10⅞"
Unsigned
Collection of Childs Gallery, Boston and New York

16.

17.

18.

19.

JAMES EDWARD BUTTERSWORTH
1817-1894

James Buttersworth was born in England in 1817 and was possibly a relative of the noted English marine painter, Thomas Buttersworth. James came to this country about 1845 and had a studio in Hoboken, New Jersey. His early years in this country were notable for the numerous portraits of majestic clipper ships he painted, many of which were reproduced as lithographs by the firm of Currier and Ives. Buttersworth paintings are often quite dramatic with stark color contrasts between the water and sky which lead the viewer to focus on the vessels he was depicting. He was a meticulous draftsman who possessed a mariner's knowledge of rigging and the setting of sails and used this effectively in his works. He died in West Hoboken, New Jersey on March 2, 1894.

20. Yacht Race Off Boston Light, *c. 1870-85*
Oil on canvas, 15⅛" x 20⅛"
Signed l.r. "J.E. Buttersworth"
Collection Peabody Museum of Salem (M16,242)

Buttersworth turned to depictions of yacht racing with the decline of the clipper ship in the years following the Civil War. This view of carefully detailed ships in a realistic marine setting is typical of the successful formula he used for the rest of his life.

CHARLES D. CAHOON
1861-1951

Charles Cahoon, a native Cape Codder, worked in a photography studio in Boston as a restorer from about 1880 until the turn of the century. It was during this period that he painted in his spare time until, at the age of forty, he decided to make it his full time occupation. He returned to the Cape and initially earned a living by painting copies of Old Masters. His later work consisted primarily of coastal views and landscapes of the Cape region. He died in 1951.

21. Cape Cod Sand Dune, *nd*
Oil on canvas, 16" x 22"
Signed l.r. "C.D. Cahoon"
Collection of Centerville Historical Society

JAMES FLOYD CLYMER
1893-(exact date unknown) 1970's

Floyd Clymer was born in Pennsylvania on March 31, 1893. He exhibited at the Pennsylvania Academy of Fine Arts in 1924 and was living in Provincetown by the end of that decade. He and his wife (the daughter of Frederick Waugh) ran a costume shop in Provincetown, in addition to his work as an artist. It is believed that he moved to upstate New York in the 1940's and died there sometime in the 1970's. Broad, flattened areas of color are typical of his work.

22. Dock in Winter, *nd*
Oil on board, 26" x 36"
Signed l.l. "Clymer"
Collection of Provincetown Art Association and Museum

20.

21.

22.

E.C. COATES
Active 1837-1867

Edmund (or Edward as as he was listed in the New York City Directory) C. Coates was a landscape, marine and historical painter. Like Thomas Chambers, Coates often worked after prints as well as originating his own compositions. Many of his works are landscapes of New York State or Italian scenes. He exhibited at the National Academy in 1841.

23. **Boston Harbor,** *1867*
    Oil on canvas, 24½" x 32½"
    Signed l.r. "E.C. Coates 1867"
    Collection of Morton Bradley

DARIUS COBB
1834-1919

Darius Cobb, the twin brother of artist Cyrus Cobb, was born in Malden, Massachusetts, August 6, 1834. Darius was primarily a portrait painter but collaborated with his brother on a number of large historical and religious paintings in addition to composing some landscapes. The two worked together from the 1850's until about 1870. Both brothers are also noted for their work in sculpture. Darius died April 23, 1919 in Newton Upper Falls, Massachusetts.

24. **After the Storm,** *1874*
    Oil on canvas, 12" x 20"
    Signed l.r. "Darius Cobb"
    Collection of a Member of Heritage Plantation
    This painting probably depicts the South Shore near Duxbury.

JOHN AMORY CODMAN
1824-1886

John Codman was born in Roxbury, Massachusetts in 1824, the son of Henry and Catherine Willard Amory Codman. He was a portrait and landscape painter working in Boston during the mid-nineteenth century and died in that city in 1886. His daughter, Martha Codman Karolik, and her husband, Maxim Karolik, formed the great collection of American art and decorative art at the Museum of Fine Arts, Boston.

25. **Shore of Marblehead Neck and Tinker's Island,** *nd*
    Oil on canvas, 11¾" x 20"
    Unsigned
    Collection of the Museum of Fine Arts, Boston, Bequest of Maxim Karolik (64.591)

23.

24.

25.

THEODORE DEMEREST COE
1866-1958

Theodore Coe, born in Suffern, New York, April 13, 1866, was a pupil of John Twatchman and attended the Carlo Rossi Academy in Paris. Coe, like his contemporary, Dodge Macknight, was a resident of the Cape Cod town of East Sandwich, Massachusetts from 1910 until 1926 when he moved to Tampa, Florida. Coe was active with many of the Boston painters including Woodbury, Tarbell and, of course, Dodge Macknight. His paintings are in much the same vein as these early impressionists, with the emphasis on light, atmosphere and color. Coe turned to restoration work after his move to Tampa, where he died at the age of 92 in 1958.

26. Cape Cod Bay, *c. 1910-1926*
Oil on canvas, 18" x 23"
Signed l.r. "Theodore Coe"
Collection of The Sandwich Historical Society and Glass Museum (82.32.4)

Many of Coe's subjects are of the Cape Cod region, where he lived from 1910-1926.

JOSEPH FOXCROFT COLE
1837-1892

The landscape painter, J. Foxcroft Cole, was born in Jay, Maine, November 9, 1837. Cole became a pupil of Charles Jacque in 1867 after serving an apprenticeship as a lithographer at J.H. Bufford & Co. in Boston. He spent the next seventeen years between Europe and America and exhibited at the Salon in Paris, The Boston Athenaeum, the National Academy and the Pennsylvania Academy. He settled in Wincester, Massachusetts in 1877 and remained there until his death in 1892.

27. Boden's Point, Marblehead, Massachusetts, *1880*
Oil on canvas, 30¼" x 36"
Signed l.l. "J. Foxcroft Cole. 1880"
Collection of Essex Institute (135,352)

Boden's Point is located on the harbor side of Marblehead Neck.

FRANCOIS B. DeBLOIS
1829-1913

Francois DeBlois was born in Canada in 1829. Little is known of his life other than he was active in the Montreal and Boston regions in the second half of the nineteenth century. He exhibited at the Boston Athenaeum from 1867-1873. He died in 1913.

28. Kelloggs Beach, *nd*
Oil on canvas, 12" x 19¼"
Signed l.r. "F.B. DeBlois/Kelloggs Beach"
Collection of Mr. Morton Bradley

26.

27.

28.

MAURITZ FREDERIK HENDRIK DE HAAS
1832-1895

Mauritz de Haas, like his countryman Albert Van Beest, was born in Rotterdam and served as Artist to the Dutch Royal Navy before coming to America in 1859. DeHaas received his artistic training at The Hague and was well known for his marine paintings. He painted several naval engagements for Admiral Farragut during the Civil War and exhibited his coastal scenes at the Boston Athenaeum and the National Academy. He was elected a member of the National Academy in 1867. His brother, William, was also a noted marine painter. de Haas died in New York City in 1895.

29. Untitled New England Coastal Scene, *nd*
Oil on canvas, 40¼" x 31¼"
Signed l.l. "MFH de Hass, N.A."
Collection of Peabody Museum of Salem (Knight Collection)

30. Whitehead, East End of Cushing Island off Portland, Maine, *nd*
Oil on canvas, 6" x 5"
Signed l.r. "de Haas"
Collection of George Walter Vincent Smith Art Museum, Springfield, Massachusetts

---

WILLIAM FREDERIK DE HAAS
1830-1880

William de Haas, older brother of Mauritz, was born in Rotterdam, Holland in 1830 and studied at The Hague. He came to America in 1854, five years before Frederick, and settled in New York City. He was a frequent exhibitor at the National Academy and established a reputation as a marine painter specializing in coastal scenes. William died at Fayal in the Azores, July 16, 1880.

31. A Dreary Day at Boone Island, Maine, *1878*
Oil on canvas, 15" x 26¼"
Signed l.r. "William F. de Haas '78"
Collection of The Cahoon Museum of American Art

29.

30.

31.

FREDERICK KNECHT DETWILLER
1882-1953

Frederick Detwiller was born in Easton, Pennsylvania, on December 31, 1882. He studied at the Ecole des Beaux Arts in Paris, the Inst. di Belle Arti of Florence and at Columbia University in New York. He is noted for his ability as an illustrator and etcher in addition to his work as a painter. He died in September, 1953.

32. Port of Noank, Conn., *1918*
Oil on canvas, 30" x 40"
Signed l.r. "F.K. Detwiller"

Collection of Mystic Seaport Museum, Inc., Mystic, Connecticut (49.2740)

JOHN F. DONALD

Nothing is known of the artist John F. Donald.

33. Newport Harbor, *1874*
Oil on canvas, 21¼" X 26¾"
Signed l.l. "J.F. Donald/Sketch 1874"

Collection of The Baltimore Museum of Art, Gift of Edgar William and Bernice Chrysler Garbish, New York (BMA 1973.92.3)

This bird's-eye view of Newport may have been copied from a print of the period. Among the numerous landmarks that are recognizable are Goat Island opposite the piers, Fort Adams at the upper left and Conanicut Island across the harbor. Many of the buildings are still standing on the waterfront.

32.

33.

THOMAS DOUGHTY
1793-1856

Thomas Doughty gained a reputation as one of the nation's foremost landscape painters in the first half of the nineteenth century. He was born in Philadelphia on July 19, 1793 and was apprenticed to a leather merchant in that city. He abandoned that trade in 1820 in favor of landscape painting. Doughty was one of the first artists in America to devote himself primarily to that genre and was soon acknowledged as one of the best painters of landscapes in the United States. His works, which were often serene, tranquil views of Pennsylvania, New York or New England, were frequently exhibited at the Pennsylvania Academy, American Academy, The Boston Athenaeum, Maryland Historical Society and several galleries in Europe. Doughty also learned lithography from the firm of John B. Pendleton in Boston and later published a periodical in Philadelphia containing many of his own lithographs. He died in New York City, July 22, 1856.

34. Seacoast, *1833*
Oil on canvas, 24¼" x 35½"
Signed l.l. "T. Doughty 1833"
Collection of Addison Gallery, Phillips Academy, Gift of Mrs. Llewelyn Howland (1967.6)

35. A View of Boston From Chelsea Landing, *c. 1835*
Oil on board, 13¾" x 20"
Unsigned
Collection of Heritage Plantation (1985.7)

CLEMENT DREW
1807-1889

Very little is known about the prolific marine painter, Clement Drew. It is believed that he was born in Kingston or Boston, Massachusetts about the year 1806-07. The Boston Directory lists him as a marine painter from the years 1838 until 1878 and it is known that he also published lithographs. Drew's paintings are typically dramatic marine views featuring ships in storm tossed seas, often with surf crashing along the shore and a lighthouse in the background. Drew worked in the Gloucester area in the 1880's and is believed to have been in Maine about 1889.

36. Castle Rock, Marblehead Neck, Line Gale, *1882*
Oil on canvas, 9" x 12"
Signed reverse "Castle Rock", Marblehead/Neck: Line Gale Sept/1882 by C. Drew
Collection of Peter and Carolyn Lynch

34.

35.

36.

OSCAR DUBOIS
1842-1911

Oscar Dubois was born in Swiebrucken, Germany, August 16, 1842. His father, George Arthur Dubois, had been an artist in the French army for seven years before moving to Germany to learn the art of lithography. The family immigrated to Philadelphia in 1849 and then to Boston in 1852. Oscar worked as an artist for the lithographic firms of J.H. Bufford & Co. and Prang and Mayer while in Boston, but moved to Fall River in 1859. He and his brother, H.W., formed their own business, H.W. Dubois and Co., in that year and continued in the chromolithographic business until about 1890. A number of family members were active in the lithography company throughout its history. Oscar died on December 21, 1911.

37. Mount Hope Bay, *nd*
Gouache and watercolor on paper, 9½" x 13½"
Signed l.l. "Oscar Dubois"
Anonymous lender

This is the original painting duplicated as a chromolithograph and published by the firm of H.W. Dubois & Co. in Fall River about 1870.

38. New England Coastal View, *nd*
Watercolor on paper, 13" x 18¾"
Signed l.l. "Oscar Dubois"
Anonymous lender

39. Sunset, Mount Hope Bay, *c. 1883-1884*
Oil on board, 7½" x 11¾"
Unsigned
Anonymous lender

This unusual view of Mount Hope Bay depicts one of the fiery red sunsets that occurred world wide following the explosion of Mount Krakatau in Indonesia on August 27, 1883.

37.

38.

39.

LEMUEL D. ELDRED
1848-1921

Lemuel Eldred, the son of a Fairhaven boat builder, was born in that Massachusetts town in 1848. He came to the attention of William Bradford who opened his studio to the youth — first in Fairhaven and later in New York. Most of Eldred's early work consisted of marine views but this changed somewhat after trips to Europe in 1880 and 1883. Mediterranean lands, scenes of Venice and landscapes of the North African desert were painted in his Boston studio after his return from these trips. He resumed marine art later in life when he returned to his native town of Fairhaven and occupied Bradford's old studio. It was at this time that he produced the well-known series of etchings of the New Bedford waterfront, featuring the decaying remnants of the once proud whaling fleet. Eldred died in 1921.

40. Fishing Settlement, *1880*
Oil on canvas, 8½" x 12½"
Signed l.l. "L.D. Eldred, 1880"
Collection of Peter and Carolyn Lynch

41. New England Coastal Scene, *1875*
Oil on canvas, 12" x 20"
Signed l.r. "L.D. Eldred 75"
Collection of Peter and Carolyn Lynch

DANIEL JEROME ELWELL
1847-1912

Jerome Elwell was born in Gloucester, Massachusetts in 1847. He studied painting at the Lowell Institute in Boston in 1868 and later opened a studio in Lawrence, Massachusetts. Starting in the year 1872, Elwell made the first of many sojourns to Europe, initially to study in Antwerp and later to visit galleries throughout England and the Continent. Elwell exhibited at the Philadelphia Exposition and numerous Boston and European galleries throughout the late nineteenth and early twentieth centuries. He died in Naples in 1912.

42. Moonlight Night - Gloucester Harbor, *1882*
Oil on canvas, 10¼" x 19"
Signed l.l. "D. Jerome Elwell 6/82"
Collection of The Cahoon Museum of American Art

The lighthouse on the left was located on Ten Pound Island and no longer exists. The one on the right is Eastern Point Light and is still standing. Another of Elwell's nocturnal paintings was exhibited at the Triennial exhibit in Antwerp and received great acclaim. It was later exhibited in Boston in 1878.

JOHN JOSEPH ENNEKING
1841-1916

John Enneking is now recognized as an important American impressionist artist but was all but forgotten for several decades after his death. He was born in Minister, Ohio, October 4, 1841 and attended Mount St. Mary's College in Cincinnati. He left school to serve in the Union forces during the Civil War and later moved to Boston to marry the daughter of a wealthy merchant. Enneking studied lithography and industrial drawing in Boston and lost a tinware manufacturing business during the depression of 1870. It was at this point that he traveled to Europe with his family to study art and became familiar with the French Impressionists and the Barbizon School. Upon his return to Boston he opened a studio on Tremont Street (and later one in Maine) and experienced a large degree of success primarily with his impressionistic landscapes of the White Mountains, Maine and other New England views. He died in Boston in 1916.

43. A Cove, Singing Beach, *1877*
Oil on canvas, 12½" x 18"
Signed l.r. "Enneking 77"
Collection of Art Complex Museum, Duxbury, Massachusetts

Singing Beach is located in Manchester, Massachusetts, south of the often depicted artist's retreat of Magnolia.

43.

40.

43.

42.

41.

PLATE I — Catalog #9

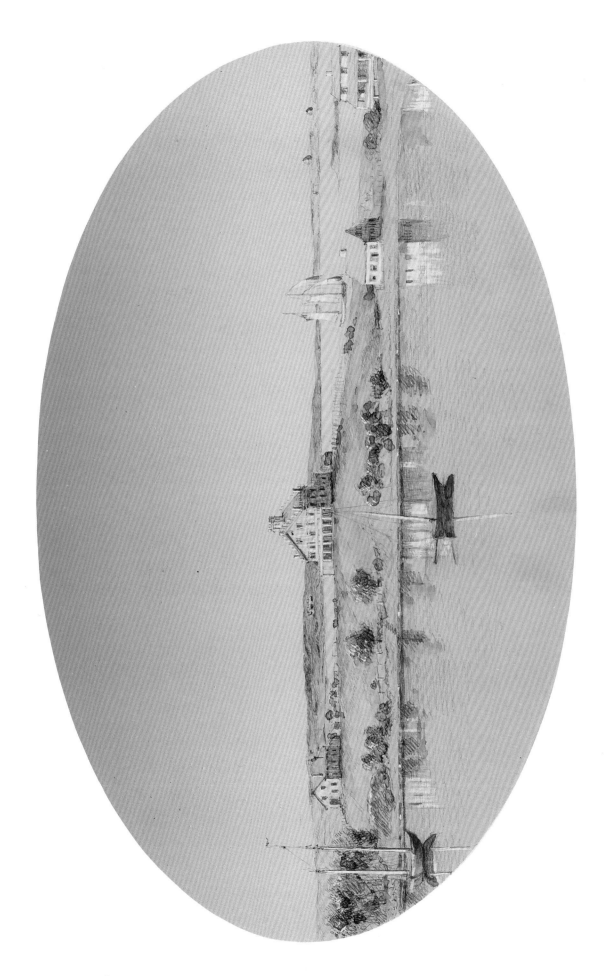

PLATE II — Catalog #47

PLATE III — Catalog #48

PLATE IV — Catalog #64

PLATE V— Catalog #65

PLATE VI — Catalog #68

PLATE VII — Catalog #71

PLATE VIII — Catalog #87

PLATE IX — Catalog #88

MARIA DENNY FAY
1820-1890

Maria Fay, the daughter of Judge Samuel Prescott Fay of Cambridge, Massachusetts, summered at Woods Hole and painted a number of panoramic views of that Cape Cod village in the late 1850's. Her brother became the first summer resident of that town after he purchased "The Homestead" in 1850. Maria very likely stayed in his home overlooking Little Harbor. Her house on Garden Street in Cambridge was the gathering sight of many of the intellectuals of the day including William James, Longfellow and James Russell Lowell. She assisted in the development of Radcliffe College and later donated her house to that institution. She died on February 15, 1890. It is not known where or how she learned to paint.

44. Church of the Messiah, Woods Hole, *c. 1854-59*
Watercolor on paper, 5¼" x 8"
Unsigned
Collection of Woods Hole Historical Society

The Church of the Messiah was built in 1854 on three acres of land donated by Maria's brother, Joseph Fay. The original building was moved and converted into the Parish House in 1888 when the present granite structure was erected. This view looks across Little Harbor from Long Neck.

45. East Cambridge From the Mill Dam, *1859*
Watercolor on paper, 5½" x 8¾"
Signed l.r. "MDF"
Collection of Woods Hole Historical Society

Other inscriptions on this painting include "East Cambridge — From the Mill Dam" and "From 119 Beacon Street/Nov. 20, 1859".
This view looks across the Charles River into Cambridge.

46. View of Woods Hole (Parkers Point), *1854-59*
Watercolor on paper, 5¼" x 8"
Unsigned
Collection of Woods Hole Historical Society

This and the following view were taken looking across Little Harbor. The Elizabeth Islands appear in the distance.

47. View From the Church Steps, Woods Hole, *1859*
Gouache on paper, 6¾" x 9¾"
Signed l.r. "View From the Church Steps about 1859/M.D.F."
Collection of Woods Hole Historical Society
Illustrated plate II

This view was taken from the steps of the Episcopal Church (No.44) looking across Little Harbor. The large building in the center was known as the Webster House. The Federal census of 1850 lists only two hundred residents of Woods Hole and thirty four homes.

44.

45.

46.

ALVIN (ALVAN) FISHER
1792-1863

Alvin Fisher, one of the pioneers of American landscape painting, was born in Needham, Massachusetts, August 9, 1792. His early training was with the portrait and ornamental painter, John Ritto Penniman of Boston and later, in 1825, he took some drawing lessons in Paris while on the Grand Tour of Europe. His first commissions were portraits but he was executing landscapes as early as 1815-1819. Sometime after this date he changed the spelling of his name from Alvin to Alvan and used this form for the rest of his life. Fisher is known to have worked in Connecticut, South Carolina, Pennsylvania and throughout New England; however, he spent the majority of his life in Boston. He died near that city in Dedham, in 1863.

48. Providence From Across the Cove, *1819*
Oil on canvas, 33¾" x 47⅝"
Signed "A. Fisher pinxt 1819"
Collection of The Rhode Island Historical Society (1905.1.1)
Illustrated plate III

Another similar painting by Fisher, done a year earlier and also in the collection of the Rhode Island Historical Society, includes a figure of a painter, probably Fisher himself. This view, looking northeast across the lower cove, was painted for the Reverend Thomas D. Carlile.

WINCKWORTH ALLAN GAY
1821-1910

W. Allan Gay was one of the best landscape painters of the late nineteenth century but is relatively unknown today. He was born in West Hingham, Massachusetts, in 1821 and took art lessons from Robert Weir as a youth. In 1847 he left for an extended tour of Europe traveling with his friend and fellow artist, Benjamin Champney. Gay was one of the very first Americans to come under the influence of the Barbizon School, which was located only forty miles southeast of Paris. There, under the study of Constant Troyon, he learned to use a looser brush work — distinct from the tightly painted landscapes of the Hudson River artists such as Thomas Durand. Gay returned to America in 1851 and opened a studio in Boston where he displayed scenes of coastal New England and the White Mountains. He exhibited at the Boston Athenaeum and the National Academy for a number of years and in the 1880's, left on a four year trip to the Far East which resulted in a large number of works, primarily of Japan.

49. Farmhouse at Rye Beach, New Hampshire, *c. 1865*
Oil on cardboard, 12" x 18"
Signed l.r. "W. Allan Gay"
Collection of The Museum of Fine Arts, Boston
Bequest of Mrs. Edward Wheelwright (13.468)

CHARLES H. GIFFORD
1839-1904

Charles Gifford is one of the lesser known landscape painters of the New Bedford school which included William Bradford, R. Swain Gifford and Lemuel D. Eldred. He was born in the neighboring town of Fairhaven, Massachusetts, and was apprenticed to a shoemaker in Middleboro. Although he had no formal artistic training, he gave up the shoemaking business in favor of landscape and marine painting in the 1860's. The work of Albert Bierstadt was influential on Gifford, and can be seen in many of his compositions. A great number of his compositions are of smaller size and usually depict the coast of New England. His paintings can best be categorized as belonging to the Luminist movement and at times show extraordinary perception of color and atmosphere. He died in Fairhaven in 1904.

50. Cliffs of No Mans Land, *1893*
Oil on canvas, 26" x 42¼"
Signed l.l. "C.H. Gifford 1893"
Collection Heritage Plantation of Sandwich (1989.7)

51. Fishing Village, *nd*
Oil on canvas, 6" x 10"
Signed l.l. "C.H. Gifford"
Collection of Peter and Carolyn Lynch

49.

50.

51.

52. Headin' Out, *1883*
Oil on canvas, 16¾" X 23¼"
Signed l.r. "C.H. Gifford-1883
Collection of Peabody Museum of Salem

53. New England Coastal Scene, *nd*
Oil on canvas, 6" x 10¼"
Signed l.r. "C.H. Gifford"
Collection of Peter and Carolyn Lynch

54. Sunset, New Bedford Harbor, *1875*
Oil on canvas, 9" x 14"
Signed l.r. "C.H. Gifford/1875"
Collection of Morton Bradley

52.

53.

54.

55. View of Fairhaven, *nd*
Oil on canvas, 5¾" x 15"
Signed l.r. "C.H. Gifford"
Collection of Mr. Morton Bradley

This grouping of works are representative of the diverse and talented style of Charles Gifford. All are attributed to either New England or perhaps Grand Manan, where Gifford briefly traveled. The "View of Fairhaven" depicts Fairhaven from the artist's home on Lafayette Street.

FRANKLIN LEWIS GIFFORD
1854-1936

Franklin Gifford was a self-taught artist from the Cape Cod town of Woods Hole. He devoted his full time to art upon his retirement as an interior decorator and house painter in 1930. The next six years, until his death in 1936, were devoted to painting historical views of the town — primarily from memory or sketches made in the nineteenth century. He exhibited one hundred and forty of these works in New York City in 1932 and published a catalogue of descriptions of the scenes. A number of the paintings were donated to the Woods Hole Library by his children after his death.

56. Waterfront at Woods Hole, *1907*
Oil on canvas, 27¼" x 66"
Signed l.r. "Sketched 1860/Painted by F.L. Gifford/1907"
Collection Woods Hole Library

This naive painting shows the steamer <u>Monohansett</u> after she has towed the whaling vessel <u>Hobomok</u> to Bar Neck Wharf. The unrigged vessel is the whaler <u>Commodore Morris</u> which was built at Woods Hole. Many of the buildings are still standing including the Candle House behind the <u>Commodore Morris.</u>

ROBERT SWAIN GIFFORD
1840-1905

R. Swain Gifford was born on the Island of Nonamesset, one of the Elizabeth Islands, which separates Buzzards Bay from Vineyard Sound, December 23, 1840. His family later moved to the town of Fairhaven where Gifford became acquainted with the marine artist, Albert Van Beest. Gifford studied under Van Beest, collaborated with him on some paintings and eventually shared a studio with him for a short period of time in New York City. Gifford traveled extensively throughout his career including trips to North Africa, Europe, Alaska, California and the Pacific Northwest. Most of his known works are marines and landscapes of the New England region, especially the Buzzards Bay area, and a large body of work detailing his travels to North Africa. He was elected an academician of the National Academy of Design in 1878 and was a founder of the New York Etching Club. Gifford died on January 15, 1905, in New York City.

57. Seconnet Rock, New Bedford, *nd*
Oil on canvas, 14¼" X 22⅛"
Signed l.l. "R. Swain Gifford"
Collection of The Brooklyn Museum, Bequest of Charles A. Schieren (15.329)

55.

56.

57.

CHARLES EDWIN LEWIS GREEN
1844-1915

C.E.L. Green was justly acclaimed during his lifetime as a noted marine and landscape artist but faded into obscurity after his death in 1915. Green was born in Lynn, Massachusetts, on April 26, 1844 and was involved in the business world for the first two decades of his adult life; however, he started painting professionally about 1879. Some documentation exists that indicates he took lessons from the artists Joshua Sheldon of Lynn and Otis Webber of Boston and possibly others. Green had opened a studio in Boston at 28 School Street by 1883 and was soon exhibiting paintings at the Massachusetts Charitable Mechanics Association, The Boston Art Club and, by 1887, at the National Academy of Design. He later made trips to Nova Scotia and Europe spending an extended period of time in the English fishing village of Newlyn. His body of known work consists primarily of local scenes of Lynn, Marblehead, Swampscott and Revere and genre scenes of Newlyn and the surrounding areas. He never dated his works, which were mostly small size canvases and was seldom interested in depicting human figures. Green remained active until 1910 and died in Lynn in 1915.

58. Swampscott, *c. 1880-90*
Oil on canvas, 17¼" x 27¼"
Signed l.r. "C.E.L. Green"
Collection of Essex Institute, Salem, Massachusetts (135,359)

59. View of Lynn, *nd*
Oil on canvas, 10" x 14"
Signed L.R. "C.E.L. Green"
Collection of Lynn Historical Society (88.40.1)

EMILE ALBERT GRUPPE
1896-1978

Emile Gruppe was born in Rochester, New York, on November 23, 1896. He was a student at the National Academy, the Art Students League and La Grande Chaumiere in Paris in addition to being a pupil of both John Carlson and Charles Hawthorne. His impressionistic marines of the Gloucester area were exhibited at the National Academy, and he was the recipient of numerous art awards. He died in Gloucester in 1978.

60. Blue Boat, *nd*
Oil on canvas, 30" x 25"
Signed l.l. "Emile A. Gruppe"
Collection of Cape Ann Historical Association (2233-1)

HENDRICKS A. HALLETT
1847-1921

Hendricks Hallett was born in Charlestown, Massachusetts in 1847 and studied in Paris and Antwerp. He was a member of the Boston Society of Watercolor Painters and was well known for his marine and ship pictures. He died in Boston in 1921.

61. Boston Harbor at Low Tide, *nd*
Watercolor on paper, 19¼" x 28⅝"
Signed l.l. "Hendricks A. Hallett"
Collection of Mystic Seaport Museum, Inc., Mystic, Connecticut (78.10)

This watercolor, showing a passing schooner in the background, a distant view of the Boston waterfront and the reflections in the water mirroring the stranded sailing vessel, is an example of Hallett at his best.

59.

61.

58.

60.

WILLIAM STANLEY HASELTINE
1835-1900

William Haseltine was born in Philadelphia June 11, 1835. His mother, Mrs. Elizabeth Stanley Haseltine, and two of his brothers, Charles and James, were all recognized artists of the nineteenth century. William took lessons from the landscape artist Paul Webber (1823-1916) and later accompanied him on a tour of Europe 1854. Haseltine studied under Andreas Achenbauch in Dusseldorf and later met and became friends with Albert Bierstadt, Thomas Worthington Whittredge and Emanuel Gottlieb Leutze. Haseltine became a member of the National Academy of Design in 1859, but chose to spend most of of his life as an expatriate in Rome. He died in that city in 1900. Haseltine made annual visits to this country and remained active in American art affairs throughout this period even serving on the art committee for the 1893 Columbian Exposition. He was also one of the founders of the American Academy in Rome.

62. After a Shower-Nahant, Massachusetts, *c. 1862*
Oil on canvas, 14⅞" x 23"
Signed l.l. "W S H" in monogram
Collection of The Brooklyn Museum, Gift of Mrs. Helen H. Plowden (48.197)

63. Castle Rock, Nahant, *1865*
Oil on canvas, 24" x 38"
Signed l.r. "W.S. Haseltine/1865"
Collection of The Corcoran Gallery of Art, Gift of Helen Haseltine Plowden

Nahant, off the coast of Lynn, was a favorite subject for many marine artists of the nineteenth century.

64. Seal Harbor, Mount Desert, Maine, *nd.*
Watercolor on paper, 14¼" x 21½"
Unsigned

Collection of Georgia Museum of Art, The University of Georgia, Gift of Mrs. Helen Plowden, Courtesy of National Academy of Design
Illustrated plate IV

Much like Kensett, Haseltine frequently made use of silhouetted rocks and contrasting light and shadow.

62.

63.

FREDERICK CHILDE HASSAM
1859-1935

Childe Hassam has long been considered one of America's foremost Impressionist painters. He was born in Dorchester, Massachusetts and started his career as an illustrator for a Boston wood engraver. He made the first of many trips to Europe in 1883, but it was during the trip to Paris in 1886 that he absorbed the fundamentals of Impressionism. That year he studied at the Academie Julian under Gustave Boulanger and Jules Lefebvre and later, in the years 1887, 1888 and 1889, showed paintings at the Paris Salon. His work as an Impressionist is most likened to that of Monets, yet is distinctly American with solid three-dimensional modeling and picturesque subjects. He was a founding member of The Ten, a group of painters who held annual shows from 1898 to 1906 in defiance to the more conservative Society of American Artists. He exhibited on numerous other occasions and was the recipient of many art awards. He died in East Hampton, New York in 1935.

65. Church at East Gloucester, *1919*
Oil on canvas, 40¾" x 51"
Signed l.l. "Childe Hassam, 1919"
Private collection
Illustrated plate V

Hassam has captured the transitory nature of light and color in this carefully composed, outstanding painting of East Gloucester and the harbor beyond.

GEORGE M. HATHAWAY
c. 1852-1903

It is believed that George Hathaway was born in Providence, Rhode Island about 1852 and that he settled in Portland, Maine around 1883. He is listed in the "Portland Directory" as a furniture decorator in 1889 and it is known that he supplied George W. Morris, a Portland publisher, with a number of marine paintings to illustrate books on Portland and Casco Bay. He returned to Providence shortly before his death in 1903.

66. Portland Head Light, *nd*
Oil on canvas, 18" x 30⅛"
Signed l.r. "GM Hathaway"
Collection of Portland Museum of Art, Gift of Union Mutual Insurance Company, 1967

The first Portland Head Light was lighted in 1791 and has been altered in various manners over the years. Hathaway painted a number of versions of this scene.

CHARLES WEBSTER HAWTHORNE
1872-1930

The founder of the Cape Cod School of Art was born in Richmond, Maine, January 8, 1872. Hawthorne was a pupil at the National Academy of Design and later a student, then teaching assistant, of William Merritt Chase at the Art Students League. After a falling out with Chase in 1898, Hawthorne founded the Cape Cod School of Art in Provincetown the following year. The clear atmosphere and a special quality of light that he found on the Cape were especially important for his method of dramatic colorful painting. He remained in Provincetown until his death in 1930.

67. Figures on a Pier, *nd*
Watercolor on paper, 10" x 14"
Unsigned
Collection of Provincetown Art Association and Museum

EDWARD HOPPER
1882-1967

Edward Hopper was one of the most talented pupils of Robert Henri. Hopper was born in Nyack, New York, July 22, 1882 and attended the New York School of Art, studying under Henri. He toured Europe three times between 1906 and 1910 and exhibited in the Armory Show of 1913. He supported himself as a commercial artist for a number of years before winning recognition as an accomplished etcher and then as an oil painter. Summers were spent in Maine until 1930 when he and his wife built a house in Truro, Massachusetts. They divided their time between New York City and the Cape for the remainder of their long lives. Hopper died in his studio in New York City in 1967. His work is best described as objective realism or representational art which features the effect of light on architectural forms.

68. Briar Neck, Gloucester, *1912*
Oil on canvas, 24" x 29"
Signed l.r. "Edward Hopper"
Collection of The Whitney Museum of American Art, Bequest of Josephine N. Hopper (70.1193)
Illustrated plate VI

Briar Neck is located on Cape Ann near Gloucester, Massachusetts.

66.

67.

JOHN BRADLEY HUDSON, JR.
1832-1903

John Hudson was a native of Portland, Maine, and worked there as a landscape and ornamental painter from the late 1850's until the late 1890's. He took art lessons from Philip Harris and from the portrait painter, Charles O. Cole; later sharing a studio in Portland with fellow artists Charles Kimball and Franklin Simmons. He briefly served in the army during the Civil War before returning to Portland where he spent the next thirty years as a successful painter. His later years were spent in Weston, Massachusetts, and South Lincoln, Massachusetts, where he died in 1903.

69. Whitehead, Cushing Island, Maine, *nd*
Oil on canvas, 26" x 38"
Signed l.r. "J.B. Hudson, Jr."

Collection of Portland Museum of Art, Purchased with gifts from Vassar College alumnae in memory of Janet Hickey Drummond, 1978

WILLIAM MORRIS HUNT
1824-1879

William Morris Hunt was born March 31, 1824 in Brattleboro, Vermont. Although he attended Harvard College for a short time, he was unable to finish due to his poor health. He left the school and went to Europe, studied at Dusseldorf for a year and in 1846 worked in the studio of Thomas Couture of Paris. Hunt met the French artist Millet through the Boston painter William Babcock and quickly became a disciple of the Barbizon School of painting. Hunt settled in Boston in 1862 and became a successful portrait painter and, with his wife, an influential advisor to collectors of art. Consequently, they were responsible for the formation of a number of excellent private collections from the Barbizon School. Hunt drowned at Appledore, one of the Isles of Shoals off the New Hampshire coast, September 8, 1879.

70. Beach Scene With Two-Horse Cart, *1874*
Oil on canvas, 15" x 24"
Signed l.l. "WMH" (Monogram)

Collection of Museum of Fine Arts, Boston, Bequest of Miss Mary Frothingham Hooper (62.179)

The horse in this picture was probably painted by Thomas Robinson (1834-1888) who was a landscape, genre and animal painter befriended by Hunt when he first came to Boston in 1865.

JONATHAN EASTMAN JOHNSON
1824-1906

Eastman Johnson, the renowned genre and portrait painter, was born in Lowell, Maine, July 29, 1824 but spent much of his early childhood in the state capitol of Augusta, where his father was Secretary of State. He briefly worked for the lithography firm of J.H. Bufford & Co. in Boston and then took up crayon portraiture back in Augusta and later in Washington, D.C. Johnson went abroad in 1849 and studied for two years at the Royal Academy in Dusseldorf and for four years at The Hague where he was known as the "American Rembrandt". On his return to America, he worked in Wisconsin, Cincinnati and Washington, D.C. until he settled permanently in New York City in 1859. His carefully composed genre scenes, especially those of Southern slavery, were immediately popular and remained so until the 1880's when his detailed style declined in popularity. His later work was devoted exclusively to portrait painting. He died in New York City on April 5, 1906.

71. Woman Reading, *c. 1874*
Oil on board, 25⅛" x 18⁹/₁₆"
Signed l.l. "E J" monogram

Collection of San Diego Museum of Art, Gift of the Gerald and Inez Grant Parker Foundation (77:09)
Illustrated plate VII

Johnson first visited the island of Nantucket in the early 1870's and made annual trips thereafter. It was on Nantucket that he painted many of his very best genre scenes, including "The Cranberry Pickers" and this great example.

CHARLES ANTON KAESELAU
1889-1970

Charles Kaeselau was born in Stockholm, Sweden, June 25, 1889. He attended the Kensington School of Art in London and the Art Institute of Chicago and from there moved to Provincetown in the early 1920's to study under Charles Hawthorne. He executed a number of murals for the WPA in Concord, Massachusetts and Lebanon, New Hampshire during the Depression and exhibited at the Newark Museum and the Philips Memorial Gallery in Washington, D.C. His professional organizations included the American Art Congress, the Provincetown Art Association and the Boston Watercolor Society. The artist died in 1970.

72. Winter, *nd*
Oil on canvas, 30" x 36"
Signed l.r. "Charles A. Kaeselau"

Collection of Provincetown Art Association & Museum

69.

70.

72.

JOHN FREDERICK KENSETT
1816-1872

John Kensett was one of the most popular landscape artists of his time. He was born in Cheshire, Connecticut, March 22, 1816 and was taught the art of engraving by his father Thomas Kensett and his uncle, Alfred Daggett of New Haven. He subsequently worked as a bank note engraver in New York City and in 1840 traveled to Europe with fellow artists Asher B. Durand, J.W. Casilear and T.P. Rossiter. Kensett studied and painted throughout England, Germany, France and Italy for the next seven years and returned to New York City in 1847. He was elected to the National Academy in 1849 and was later a member of the Board of the Metropolitan Museum. He made frequent trips to the New England coast, especially the Newport region, and the White Mountains in search of subject matter for his luminist paintings. Kensett employed very transparent glazes which help suggest the pneumatoscopic image of nature balanced against the sharp, detailed masses of the land. Kensett died unexpectedly in 1872.

73. Seascape With Schooner-Narragansett Bay, *1862*
Oil on canvas, 10⅛" x 18"
Signed l.r. "F.K. 62"

Collection of Sterling and Francine Clark Art Institute, Williamstown, Massachusetts (71.50)

This painting is an example of Kensett's favored composition consisting of a large rock mass to one side balanced by an almost empty expanse of sky and water on the other.

JOHN ROSS KEY
1832-1920

John Ross Key, grandson of the author of the "Star Spangled Banner", was born in Hagerstown, Maryland, July 16, 1832. He studied art in Paris and Munich prior to setting up a studio in Boston, Massachusetts. Key served with the Corps of Engineers during the Civil War and recorded the siege of Charleston, South Carolina in 1863. He returned to his Boston studio after the war and opened another in New York City. He exhibited at the National Academy, the Pennsylvania Academy and the Boston Athenaeum. Key died in Baltimore on March 24, 1920.

74. Marblehead Harbor, Mass., *nd*
Oil on canvas, 22¾" x 36¾"
Signed l.l. "John R. Key"
Collection of Peabody Museum of Salem (M13,691)

73.

74.

FITZ HUGH LANE
1804-1865

Fitz Hugh Lane is today considered one of the most important marine and landscape artists of the nineteenth century. Lane, who was born in Gloucester, Massachusetts, December 18, 1804, began his artistic career as an apprentice to the important lithographic firm of William Pendleton in Boston in 1832. He was painting his first oils by 1840 and was listed in the Boston Almanac of 1841 as a "marine painter" residing at 17 School Street. Lane was in partnership with another noted marine painter, John W.A. Scott, from 1845 to 1847, painting marine views of Gloucester and Boston Harbors in the manner of Robert Salmon. Lane returned to Gloucester in 1849 and remained there for the rest of his life except for his annual summer trips (especially to the Maine coast) in search of topics for his canvases. Many of Lane's paintings exhibit spectacular atmospheric effects achieved, in part, by the introduction in the 1850's of new synthetic pigments. Lane died in Gloucester on August 13, 1865.

75. Clipper Ship "Southern Cross" Leaving Boston Harbor, *1851*
Oil on canvas, 25¼" x 38"
Signed l.r. "F.H. Lane. 1851"
Collection Peabody Museum of Salem

This painting is an excellent example of the mastery and detailed knowledge Lane had of ships rigging and sails in addition to demonstrating his predilection of attention to background composition.

75.

WILLIAM H. LITTLEFIELD
1902-1969

William Littlefield studied with Hans Hoffman and at the Fogg Museum in Boston. After graduating from Harvard University in 1924, he went on an extended tour of Europe, returning in 1930. His work, mostly of Cape Cod scenes, is well represented in many university museums, the Museum of Fine Arts, Boston and the Worcester Art Museum. He died in Woods Hole, Massachusetts in 1969.

76. Saconnessett Hills, *1930*
Oil on canvas, 32" x 55"
Signed on reverse "William H. Littlefield/Saconnessett Hills/1930"
Collection of Woods Hole Historical Society

A note on the reverse of this painting reads "View from the Cape Codder Hotel." The Cape Codder was located in West Falmouth and looked out on Buzzards Bay.

DODGE MACKNIGHT
1860-1950

Dodge Macknight was born in Providence, Rhode Island, October 1, 1860. The son of a silversmith, he grew up in modest circumstances and, as a boy, began his art career painting for amateur theatricals. His early adulthood was spent working for various theater and opera groups and, for a time, Taber Art Company. In 1884 Macknight traveled to France and studied at the Atelier Common in Paris. After completing four years of training, Macknight spent the next several years touring Europe and North Africa. He settled in the Cape Cod town of East Sandwich in 1897 and found the ensuing years to be productive and profitable artistically. His growing circle of enthusiastic supporters and fellow artists included Isabella Stuart Gardiner, John Singer Sargent and Denman Ross. Many successful art shows followed, peaking in the year 1923. Unfortunately, Macknight decided to stop painting after the premature death of his son, John, in 1928. Gardening became his chief interest until his own death in 1950.

77. Sand Dunes — Provincetown, *nd*
Watercolor on paper, 16" x 22¼"
Signed l.l. "Dodge Macknight"
Collection Sandwich Historical Society and Glass Museum (82.35.7)

ROSS E. MOFFETT
1888-1971

Ross Moffett was born into a farm family in Clearwater, Iowa on February 18, 1888. He was a pupil of the Art Students League of New York and studied at The Art Institute of Chicago for three years. Moffett decided to travel to the art colony at Provincetown, Massachusetts after viewing the "revolutionary" Armory Show and subsequently decided to live in that town year round after his marriage in 1920. He was elected a Member of the National Academy in 1942 and was commissioned by them to paint murals at the Eisenhower Memorial Museum in Abilene, Kansas. Moffett died March 13, 1971.

78. Marine Disaster, *1939*
Oil on canvas, 30" x 48"
Signed l.r. "Ross Moffett"
Collection of Provincetown Art Association and Museum

This painting most probably depicts the havoc wrecked by the 1938 hurricane on the Cape Cod shore.

76.

77.

78.

EDWARD MORAN
1829-1901

Edward Moran was the oldest of three brothers who were born in Lancashire, England and who all became noted artists after moving to the United States in 1844. Edward Moran was born August 19, 1829 and was initially trained to become a weaver. After his family moved to Maryland, Edward took painting lessons in Philadelphia from Paul Weber and James Hamilton and was in partnership with his brother Thomas by 1857. The two of them returned to England for further study in 1862 and by 1872, Edward was established in New York City where he remained for the rest of his life. He is particularly noted for his Turner-like seascapes as is his better known younger brother, Thomas. Edward died in New York City on June 9, 1901.

79. Casco Bay, Coast of Maine, *c. 1889*
Oil on canvas, 20" x 26"
Signed l.l. "Edw. Moran"
Collection of Heckscher Museum, Huntington, New York, Gift of August Hecksher

80. Off the Coast of Maine, *nd*
Oil on canvas, 16" x 23½"
Unsigned
Collection of a member of Heritage Plantation

79.

80.

EDWIN W. NICHOLS
date unknown

Nothing is known about the artist Edwin W. Nichols other than the appearance of his name in the Providence City Directory in the years 1872, 1873, 1875 and 1877-1879; first as a "painter" and for 1879 as a "paper hanger".

81. Southwest View of Providence Looking up Narragansett Bay, *1870*
Oil on canvas, 30" X 49½"
Signed l.l. "E.W. Nichols 1870"

Collection of The Rhode Island Historical Society (1973.67.1)

This view of Providence, looking up the bay, is the only known work by Nichols. The towers of the Rhode Island Hospital are seen at the far left of the painting.

CHARLES PARSONS
1821-1910

Charles Parsons was a noted lithographer and marine painter who was born in Hampshire, England on May 8, 1821. His family moved to America and settled in New York City when he was nine years old. Three years later he was apprenticed to the lithographic firm of Endicott & Co. and was soon taken on as a regular employee. It was during this period that Parsons executed a number of lithographs for Currier and Ives. From 1861 until his retirement in 1889, he was the head of the art department of Harper & Brothers. Parsons was an accomplished painter in addition to his lithography work and was elected as an Associate of the National Academy in 1862. He died in Brooklyn on November 9, 1910.

82. Marblehead Morning, *1884*
Oil on canvas, 14¾" x 25⅞"
Signed l.l. "Charles Parsons, 1884"

Collection of Peabody Museum of Salem (Knight Collection)

This painting depicts Lovis Cove, Marblehead, when tourism was well on its way to becoming the predominant industry in that town. The large summer homes on the bluffs attest to the rise of the popularity of that picturesque community.

81.

82.

ARTHUR PARTON
1842-1914

Arthur Parton was born at Hudson, New York, March 26, 1842. He studied in Philadelphia under William Trost Richards before visiting Europe in 1869. This trip through Britain and France was to have considerable impact on his technique. The effects of the Barbizon School, in particular his contact with Corot and Millet, are evident in his subsequent works. He was elected a National Academician in 1884 and was a member of the American Watercolor Society. He died in Yonkers, New York, March 7, 1914.

83. Misty Morning, Coast of Maine, *nd*
Oil on canvas, 9¼" x 17¼"
Signed l.l. "AP" (monogram)
Collection of the Brooklyn Museum (06.31) Bequest of Mrs. Caroline H. Polhemus

---

WILLIAM POLLARD
Active c. 1850

Nothing is known of the artist William Pollard.

84. Ship Constitution in Boston Harbor, *1846*
Oil on canvas, 18" x 26"
Unsigned

Collection of The Bostonian Society (1887.147)

A note on the back reads "This picture of the U.S. Frigate Constitution (Old Ironsides) was made from a sketch of her as she lay in Boston Harbor in the year 1846, after returning from a cruise around the world under the command of Captain John Percival. It is now presented to the Bostonian Society by the undersigned who was on board of her as Captain's clerk for the year 1843-1846. (Signed) Benjamin F. Stevens" Captain John (Mad Jack) Percival was a Cape Cod native and is buried in West Barnstable, Massachusetts.

ARTHUR QUARTLEY
1839-1886

Arthur Quartley was the son of Frederick Quartley, a wood engraver noted for his work "Picturesque America" and "Picturesque Europe". Arthur was born in France in 1839 and came to this country with his father in 1851. They settled in New York City where Arthur became a sign painter and later an accomplished marine painter. He was elected an Associate of the National Academy in 1879 and an Academician in 1886, the year of his death.

85. Casewell's Peak, Isles of Shoals, *nd*
Oil on canvas, 19" x 35½"
Unsigned (attributed)

Collection of Peabody Museum of Salem (M8562)

Relatively few paintings were done of the New Hampshire coastline since it is only 131 miles in length. The Isles of Shoals are a group of nearly barren islands that lie about nine miles off the coast.

83.

84.

85.

WILLIAM TROST RICHARDS
1833-1905

The noted marine artist, William Trost Richards, was initially a designer of gas fixtures before becoming interested in painting. Richards was born in Philadelphia, November 14, 1833 and studied art under Paul Weber before departing in 1853 for three years of study in Florence, Rome and Paris. After his return in 1856, he settled in Germantown, Pennsylvania, and painted landscapes and still lifes which are characterized by an extraordinary concern for detail. By 1867, however, he began to specialize in marines which were more given to the effects of light, atmosphere and the grandeur of nature. Richards visited Newport, Rhode Island in 1874 and moved there in 1890. He died November 8, 1905.

86. Off the South Shore, *1896*
Oil on canvas, 20½" x 32¼"
Signed l.l. "W. T. Richards 96"
Collection of The Newport Art Museum (922.002) (Not in exhibit after September 15)

ROBERT SALMON
c. 1775-c. 1842

The work of the English born marine painter, Robert Salmon, was to have a marked effect on American artists for several decades following his departure from the United States around 1842. It is believed that Salmon was born about 1775 possibly in the port of Whitehaven, England. His early career, from 1800-1827, was spent painting city and harbor views of Scotland and England in the English tradition established by Canaletto and Samuel Scott. He arrived in Boston in 1828 and found considerable success with his paintings of that harbor and the surrounding environs. Salmon undoubtedly influenced a number of younger artists including William Bradford, Albert Van Beest and Fitz Hugh Lane, whose paintings exhibit striking similarity of style, crispness and composition. Salmon apparently returned to Scotland about 1842 and died soon after.

87. Chelsea Creek, *1832*
Oil on panel, 19⅜" x 27⅛"
Signed on reverse "no. 735 Painted by R. Salmon 1832"
Collection of the Peabody Museum of Salem (M11,007)
Illustrated plate VII

This view of the ferry landing and shoreline was commissioned by Henry Sigourney of Chelsea, a director of the Chelsea Ferry Company. Sigourney's house is on the slope in the background.

JOHN WHITE ALLEN SCOTT
1815-1907

John Scott, Nathaniel Currier and Fitz Hugh Lane all served apprenticeships with the Boston lithography firm of William Pendleton. Scott and Lane later formed their own lithographic firm and were partners from 1845-1847. Scott was born in Roxbury in 1815 and remained in the Boston region all his life. He exhibited at the Boston Athenaeum a number of times in the mid-nineteenth century. Scott died in Cambridge on March 4, 1907.

88. Boston Harbor, *1853*
Oil on canvas, 38½" x 50½"
Signed l.r. "J.W.A. Scott Pt"
Collection of The Bostonian Society (1884.209)
Illustrated plate IX

This view of Boston harbor was painted for an engraving printed by J. H. Bufford. It shows a relatively uncluttered harbor with most of the activity taking place on Broad Street, near the site of the Boston Tea Party. Many of the warehouses in this view were demolished in 1868 when Atlantic Avenue was laid out.

89. Boston Harbor, *nd*
Oil on canvas, 20¾" x 30"
Unsigned (in the manner of Scott)
Collection of a member of Heritage Plantation

This view of Boston Harbor shows a White Diamond Line packet leaving the harbor.

FRANCIS AUGUSTUS SILVA
1835-1886

Francis Silva exhibited pen drawings at the American Institute in New York City as a boy in 1848-1850. He was born in that city in 1835 and worked as a sign painter before serving in the Union forces during the Civil War. He took up marine painting as a career after the war, executing luminist views of the coast from the Chesapeake Bay to the New England shores. He became a member of the Watercolor Society in 1872 and exhibited eighteen times at the National Academy between 1868 and when he died in 1886.

90. A September Day on the Coast, *1879*
Oil on canvas, 20" x 38"
Signed l.l. "Francis A. Silva/'79" and on reverse "A September Day on the Coast/Francis A. Silva"
Collection of Peter and Carolyn Lynch

This painting is a view of the coast of Point Judith, Rhode Island.

86.

89.

90.

JOHN SLOAN
1871-1951

Few artists were as successful as John Sloan in chronicling urban life of the early twentieth century. Sloan, who was born in Lock Haven, Pennsylvania on August 2, 1871, started his career as an illustrator on the Philadelphia Inquirer when he was twenty-one years old. In this environment, he became acquainted with George Luks, Everitt Shinn, Robert Henri and William Glackens. He studied at the Philadelphia Academy and later, with the encouragement of Robert Henri (the founder of the Ashcan School), exhibited his paintings in 1908. Sloan spent the summers from 1914 through 1918 teaching and painting in Gloucester and in later years, in the southwest. Sloan is probably best remembered for his New York scenes of ordinary people and their haunts; a shocking theme to the art critics of the early twentieth century. The free brush strokes and bright colors of the post-impressionists characterize much of Sloan's work. He died in Gloucester in 1951.

91. Gloucester Harbor, *1916*
Oil on canvas, 26" x 32"
Signed l.r. "John Sloan"
Collection of The Syracuse University Art Collection

Ashcan School is the term used to describe the work of The Eight which dwelt primarily on everyday backyard scenes, rooftops, industry and night life. This painting of Gloucester Harbor emphasizes the cranes, factory buildings, wharves, fishing boats and other commercial activity common to ports throughout New England but seldom depicted in paintings.

FRANK VINING SMITH
1879-1967

Frank Vining Smith was born in Whitman, Massachusetts on August 25, 1871. He studied under Frank Benson, Philip Hale and Edmund Tarbell at the School of the Museum of Fine Arts in Boston and was later employed on the art staff of several Boston papers and journals. He decided to become a full time marine artist around the year 1925, consequently quit his job and found employment as an artist for numerous yacht clubs and yachtsmen. Smith was well established as a marine artist by the 1940's and continued to paint almost until his death in 1967.

92. After the Storm, *nd*
Oil on board, 23¼" x 31¼"
Signed l.r. "Frank Vining Smith"
Anonymous lender

HENRY PEMBER SMITH
1854-1907

Henry Smith was a New England landscape painter born in Waterford, Connecticut on February 20, 1854. He was a member of the American Watercolor Society and The Artist's Fund Society of New York. He died in Ashbury Park, New Jersey, October 16, 1907.

93. Village Landscape, *1881*
Oil on canvas, 10¹⁵/₁₆" x 14⁵/₁₆"
Signed l.l. "Henry P. Smith 1881"
Collection of The Sterling and Francine Clark Art Institute, Williamstown, Massachusetts

91.

92.

93.

MAURICE STERNE
1878-1957

Maurice Sterne was born in Libau, (Latvia) Russia and came to this country in 1890 at the age of twelve. He studied at the National School of Design and with Thomas Eakins and at Coopers Union. His work shows the influence of the French artists Manet and Cezanne. Sterne taught at the California School of Fine Arts from 1934 through 1936 and worked in Provincetown throughout the years 1915-1947. Sterne was a member of the National Academy of Design and was the recipient of numerous awards during his career until his death in 1957.

94. Untitled (Scow in Harbor), *nd*
Oil on board, 16" x 20"
Signed l.r. "Sterne"
Collection of Provincetown Art Association and Museum

WILLIAM LESTER STEVENS
1888-1969

Lester Stevens was one of the founders of the Rockport Art Association in 1921. Stevens, who was born in Rockport, June 15, 1888, studied with Parker Perkins at an early age and received a scholarship to the School of the Museum of Fine Arts in Boston. He returned to Rockport in 1921 after service in the army and, with fifty other artists, formed the Rockport Art Association. Stevens taught art in Rockport, Boston University and Princeton in addition to his work as a painter. He frequently traveled the New England coast in search of subjects for his paintings, ranging as far north as Grand Manan Island.

95. Driftwood, *nd*
Oil on canvas, 21" x 36"
Signed l.l. "W. Lester Stevens N.A."
Courtesy Childs Gallery, Boston and New York

ANTONIO JOHANNES THIEME
1888-1954

Anthony Thieme was born in Rotterdam, Holland on February 20, 1888. He studied at the Royal Academy of Holland and didn't come to this country until the 1920's. He settled in Rockport, Massachusetts and was one of the founding members of the Rockport Art Association in addition to being a member of the Boston Watercolor Society, New York Watercolor Society, North Shore Art Association and the Providence Watercolor Club. He had a highly successful art school from 1930 until 1942 and was elected to the National Academy in 1934. Although he was quite successful as a marine artist he was unhappy with his personal life and committed suicide in 1954.

96. Rockport Harbor, *nd*
Oil on canvas, 21" x 29½"
signed, l.l. "A Thieme"
Collection of a member of Heritage Plantation

ROSS STERLING TURNER
1847-1915

Ross Turner was born in Westport, New York in 1847. His artistic career began after 1873 and by 1876 he was touring and studying in Europe, primarily in Germany and Italy. He was a professor at Normal Art School in Boston by 1909 and was known for his work both in oils and as an illustrator. He died in 1915.

97. The Last Haven, *1880*
Oil on canvas, 30" x 45"
Signed l.r. "Ross Turner 1880"
Collection of Essex Institute (106,733)

This view of Boston Harbor shows the "U.S.S. Niagara" at her berth prior to being dismantled.

94.

95.

96.

97.

ALBERT VAN BEEST
1820-1860

The Dutch marine painter, Albert Van Beest, reportedly came to this country about 1845 and moved to Fairhaven at the invitation of William Bradford in 1854. The few short years that Van Beest spent in that whaling port were instrumental in influencing the style of marine painting seen in the works of Bradford and Robert Swain Gifford, another of Van Beests' pupils. Van Beest was born in Rotterdam and trained in the manner of the Dutch marine painters who worked in the luminist style. He sailed and painted with the Dutch Navy for several years before coming to this country and eventually sharing a studio with Bradford. Van Beest moved to New York City in 1857 and died there three years later.

98. Nahant Hotel, *1854*
Oil on canvas, 27" x 39¼"
Signed l.r. "Albert Van Beest 1854"

Collection of The Lynn Historical Society (2022)

BEATRICE (WHITNEY) VAN NESS
1888-1981

Beatrice Van Ness was born in Chelsea, Massachusetts and studied under Tarbell, Benson (who was later a neighbor in Maine), Hale and Pratt at the School of the Museum of Fine Arts, Boston and later under Charles Woodbury for a summer in Ogunquit. She founded the art department at the Beaver County Day School in Chestnut Hill in 1921 and taught there until 1949. Most of her summers were spent in Maine where she often worked with Benson and experimented with the effects of direct sunlight and reflection. Her works in this period show she placed far more importance on color and design than on the subject matter. Van Ness died in Brookline, Massachusetts in 1981.

99. Dizzy Heights, *1925-26*
Oil on canvas, 60" x 40"
Unsigned

Collection of Childs Gallery, Boston and New York

This painting depicts the artist's two daughters, Sylvia and Mary playing on "Posing Rock," North Haven, Maine. The affinity Van Ness shares with Benson and Woodbury are readily apparent in this painting in which color and light play such an important role.

98.

99.

FREDERICK JUDD WAUGH
1861-1940

Frederick Waugh's parents were both artists; his father a landscape and portrait painter and his mother a miniaturist. He was born in Bordentown, New Jersey, September 13, 1861 and attended the Pennsylvania Academy of Fine Arts and the Julian Academy in Paris. Waugh studied under Eakins in Philadelphia and Bouguereau while in Paris. He later had studios in various places in Europe from 1892-1907. He died in Provincetown in 1940.

100. Untitled (Seascape), *nd*
Oil on canvas, 25½" x 35½"
Signed l.r. "Waugh"
Collection of Provincetown Art Association and Museum

Waugh was noted for his realistic scenes of crashing waves and the churning motion and energy of the sea.

CHARLES HERBERT WOODBURY
1864-1940

Charles Woodbury approached art with a scientific curiosity. His fascination with motion and force was apparent in the manner in which he depicted the ocean on his canvases. Woodbury graduated from MIT in 1886 with a degree in engineering but quickly turned to art as a profession. He established an artist's colony at Ogunquit, Maine in 1888 which would eventually include such gifted students as Gertrude Fiske and Mabel Woodward. His innovative approach to painting relied more on color, light and patterns than on form. This is often seen in his work where free brushwork reduces landscapes to broad, flat bands of color. His seascapes emphasize the constant movement and change to be found on the ocean and the crashing surf. Woodbury continued to paint and teach until his death in 1940.

101. Saugus River, *c. 1885*
Oil on canvas, 16¼" x 26¼"
Unsigned
Collection of Lynn Historical Society

102. Shore Scene at Ogunquit, *nd*
Oil on canvas, 20" x 27"
Signed l.r. "Char. H. Woodbury"
Collection of a member of Heritage Plantation

It is believed that this is an area of Ogunquit called The Marginal Way which was especially difficult to depict on canvas.

100.

101.

102.

MABEL MAY WOODWARD
1877-1945

One of Charles Woodbury's most gifted students was Mabel Woodward. She was born in Providence, Rhode Island, September 28, 1877 and was a pupil of William Merritt Chase, Frank Vincent DuMond and Kenyon Cox in addition to her association with Woodbury at the Ogunquit Art Association. She taught at the Rhode Island School of Design for a quarter of a century and summered in Ogunquit where she painted many of her colorful impressionistic scenes for which she is best known. She died in Providence in 1945.

103. Ogunquit Beach, *nd*
Oil on canvas, 16" x 20"
Unsigned
Collection of Mr. Morton Bradley

Unidentified Artists

104. Field's Point, *c. 1875-85*
Oil on canvas, 16⅛" x 32"
Unsigned
Collection of The Rhode Island Historical Society (1933.6.1)

This painting depicts a Rhode Island clambake at Field's Point on the west shore of the Providence River during the late nineteenth century. Three other similar versions of this painting exist by the same hand — extraordinary subject matter for the nineteenth century painter.

105. View From Lovers Leap, *c. 1850*
Gouache on paper, 19½" x 29½"
Unsigned
Collection of The Lynn Historical Society

This panoramic view from Lovers Leap overlooks the pre-industrial city of Lynn into Nahant Bay. Many of the structures in the painting are still standing.

106. Boston From East Boston Ferry Slip, *c. 1835-40*
Oil on canvas, 15⅛" x 20⅛"
Unsigned
Collection of The Bostonian Society (1984.8.1)

This painting is done in the style of Charles Hubbard (1801-1876).

104.

106.

103.

105.

ACKNOWLEDGMENTS

An exhibit of this nature is possible only by the cooperation, generosity and hard work of scores of people. We are most grateful to Peter and Carolyn Lynch of Marblehead and Franklin Graphics of Providence for their financial assistance towards the publication of this catalogue.

I also wish to thank the Directors, Trustees and staff of all the lending institutions and all the collectors and galleries that were so willing to participate in this venture. Additionally, the following people bear special mention for their assistance and contribution to this project: Martha Adams, Leigh Albritton, Martha Asher, Martha Adkins Blakeslee, Paul Bourcier, Russell Bowman, Morton Bradley, David Brooke, Richard A. Bourne Co., Inc., Philip Budlong, Lucy J. Butler, Michele Butterfield, Elizabeth Codding, Dr. Alfred T. Collette, Allison Cwyin, Joel P. Davis, William R. Davis, Mr. and Mrs. Laurent Dubois, Jr. and family, Anita Dutette, Linda Eppich, William Evaul, Robert D. Farwell, Benjamin Fuller, Mrs. Natalie Freeman, Jennifer Stone Gaines, Barbara Dyer Gallati, Sophie Garrett, Louis Goldich, Maria A. Hall, Laura L.V. Hardin, Melanie Harwood, Heather Haskell, Martha Hoppin, Lynne M. Horton, D. Roger Howlett, Catherine Hunter, Sonia Johnston, Franklin Kelly, Steven Kern, Donald Keyes, Susan Larson, Ellen W. Lee, Wynn Lee, Mrs. George Lynch, Peter and Carolyn Lynch, Ned Manter, Dianne Marshall, Julian McDonough, James Mundy, Nancy Lee Nelson, Anna C. Noll, Martha Oaks, Susan Olney, Thomas Wendall Parker, Harriet Pemstein, Martin E. Peterson, David L. Prince, Richard A. Rowe, Dr. R.M. Rowe, Martha Severins, Clyde Singer, Theodore E. Stebbins, Jr., Maggie Stier, Judith Tacelli, Nicki Thiras, William Tiyus, Kenneth C. Turino, Maureen Twohig, Linda Waites, Robert K. Weis, Charles Weyerhaeuser, Paul Winfisky and James Zimmerman.

As always, the assistance of the staff at Heritage Plantation was essential to the success of mounting a loan exhibit of this scope. In particular, the skills and patience of Alotta Whitney, Registrar, and the assistance of Alfred Andre, Bill Brock, James Cervantes, Phil Dolan, Tom Guest, Jim Harwick, Beverly Jacobs, Virginia Long, Don Manchester, Dianne Marshall, Pat Rogers, Sandie Simpson and Nancy Tyrer are especially appreciated.

My wife, Nancy, merits special recognition for her contributions, patience and assistance which were essential to my sanity and the success of this endeavor.

Finally, I would like to thank the Director, Gene A. Schott, and the Museum's Trustees, for their support, without which, this exhibit would not be possible.

Brian Cullity, *Curator, Art Museum*

PHOTO CREDITS

(numbers refer to catalogue entries)
George M. Cushing, 3
Ricard Eells, 1
Ned Manter, 6, 9, 12, 13, 14, 15, 16, 17, 18, 19, 21, 23, 26, 28, 31, 35, 36, 37, 38, 39, 40, 41, 42, 44, 45, 46, 47, 50, 51, 53, 54, 55, 56, 61, 77, 78, 81, 91, 92, 94, 97, 101, 105
Dianne Marshall, 24, 43, 98, 104
Micheal McKelvey, 65
Mark Sexton, 27, 59, 99
Mary Anne Stets Photo, Mystic Seaport, Mystic, CT, 32
Claire White-Peterson photo, Mystic Seaport, Mystic, CT, 62
All others courtesy of lending institutions

BIBLIOGRAPHY

Czestochowski, Joseph S., *"The American Landscape Tradition"*, (Exhibition Catalogue), New York; E.P. Dutton, Inc., 1982

diCurcio, Robert A., *"Art on Nantucket"*, Nantucket Historical Association; Nantucket, 1982

Driscoll, John Paul and John H. Howat, *"John Frederick Kensett: An American Master"* (Exhibition Catalogue), Worcester Art Museum, Worcester, 1985

Fairbrother, Trevor J., *"The Bostonians: Painters of an Elegant Age 1870-1930"* (Exhibition Catalogue) Museum of Fine Arts, Boston, 1986

Goodrich, Lloyd, *"Edward Hopper"*. New York; Harry N. Abrams, Inc, nd

Groce, George C. and David H. Wallace, *"The New York Historical Society's Dictionary of American Artists in America"*, New Haven; Yale University Press, 1957, 1966

Hall, Elton W., *"R. Swain Gifford 1840-1905"* (Exhibition Catalogue), Old Dartmouth Historical Society, 1974

Howat, John K. et al, *"The Hudson River and its Painters"*, New York; Viking Press, 1972

Johnston, Paul Forsythe, *"The New England Fisheries"* (Exhibition Catalogue), Peabody Museum of Salem, Salem, 1984

Kuchta, Ronald A., *"Provincetown Painters"* (Exhibition Catalogue), Everson Museum of Art, Syracuse, NY, 1977

Maass, R. Andrew et al, *"At the Water's Edge"* (Exhibition Catalogue), Tampa Museum of Art, Tampa, FL, 1989

McLanathan, Richard, *"The American Tradition in the Arts"*, New York; Harcourt, Brace & World, Inc., 1968

Optiz, Glenn B., Editor, *"Mantle Fielding's Dictionary of American Painters, Sculptors and Engravers"*, Poughkeepsie; Apollo Book, 1986

Prown, Jules D., *"American Painting From its Beginnings to the Armory Show"*, Cleveland; The World Publishing Co., 1969

Robinson, Malcolm, *"The American Vision: Landscape Paintings of the United States"*, New York; Portland House, 1988

Schott, Gene A., *"Images of the Land: 200 Years of Landscape Painting in Northeastern America"* (Exhibition Catalogue), Heritage Plantation, Sandwich, 1983

Seamans, Joan Loria and Warren A., *"Earth, Sea and Sky: Charles Woodbury"* (Exhibition Catalogue), The MIT Museum, Cambridge, 1988

Stebbins, Theodore E. Jr., *"American Master Drawings and Watercolors"*, New York; Harper & Row, 1976

Schweizer, Paul D., *"Edward Moran"* (Exhibition Catalogue), Delaware Art Museum, Wilmington, 1979

Williams, William James, *"A Heritage of American Paintings From the National Gallery of Art"*, Maplewood, NJ; Rutledge Press, 1981

Wilmerding, John, *"American Marine Painting"*, New York; Harry N. Abrams, Inc., 1968, 1987

Wilmerding, John, *"American Light: The Luminist Movement 1850-1875"*, (Exhibition Catalogue), National Gallery of Art, Washington, D.C., 1980

Wilton, Andrew, *"J.M.W. Turner: His Art and Life"*, Secaucus, NJ; Poplar Books, 1979